tHe
JOURNEY
tO
MARRIAGE

THE
JOURNEY
TO
MARRIAGE

PRISCILLA ASAMOAH

THE JOURNEY TO MARRIAGE

Priscilla Asamoah Baffour
December 2017

Page Layout by:
Bonnah Joseph
Printing by:
PAULINES INNOVATIONS

For more information about the book and other motivational products from the author as well as special booking for seminars and symposiums, contact her on;
Hotlines: 0248503806
0203710328

Published by
PAULINES INNOVATIONS, GHANA
Tel: 0245213055, 0240553685

ACKNOWLEDGMENTS

If God is on my side, what is impossible? Nothing! I thank God so much for His wisdom, power, strength, grace and the unmerited favour I've received to write this book. I thought I wouldn't make it but by His spirit I've pushed through.

To my Spiritual mother Mrs Joy Amankwa: May God richly increase you every day.

I would like to express my heartfelt gratitude to my parents, Mr. and Mrs. BaffourAsamoah, for their love and immense support that aided me in making this book a reality.

To all my siblings, Pokuaa, Princess, Phyllis, Mummy, Frank, Mrs. Shodimu, Bernice, Samuel, Evans and all my family members: I am so thankful for your motivation and encouragement. I love you so much.

I also say a very big thank you to my Godparents, Mr. and Mrs. AddoDanso for their love, care, advice and motivation. I love you so much.

To Phebe Abugri, I say God bless you. You have really inspired me with your advice, encouragement and support.

To my one and only uncle, El-Shaddai: What can I say? I really appreciate what you've done in my life. God make you a blessed person and make you impact many generations.

To my special grandmothers, Madam AmaSerwah and Madam Sarah Okyere: God bless you both for being there for me always.

All my best childhood memories were spent with this two precious people: Mr. and Mrs. Nyarko Mensa. I am really grateful mum and dad. Thank you Dada Kofi for always checking up on me and making sure I am on the right path. I am most grateful.

Special thanks to Dorcas Beauty, AmaSaah and Ama Foriwah.

To my Personal Assistant, Abigail Amoah, God bless you richly.

To all my friends and everybody who made this book possible.

God bless you very much.

CONTENTS

ACKNOWLEDGEMENTS
INTRODUCTION
DEDICATION

HOW TO READ THIS BOOK

This book has been designed to help you in your choice of a life partner through whom you can both fulfil the plan or purpose God has for your life.

Let me be quick to say for a fact that, the concepts in this book cannot be absorbed by casual browsing or by gulping the whole book down in one reading. It should be read slowly and carefully, one chapter at a time. Do not move to the next chapter until you are sure you understand every concept in the previous chapter.

Use this as a workbook. Use highlighter as you read and mark those words or sentences or paragraphs that seem vital or especially applicable to you. As you read, discuss the concepts in each chapter with your relatives or a close friend. A second opinion from someone who knows your strengths and weakness can be especially helpful.

INTRODUCTION

"The Journey to Marriage" is a great piece put together by Ms. Priscilla AsamoahBaffour. Though not married, I have been able to put down some thought provoking ideas as a guide to the unmarried and the married alike. It focuses on pre-marital relationships.

This book is written in a very characteristic way not only to give the reader a good understanding of the subject matter but to also provide an orderly presentation of the idea of pre-marital relationship. This would help young people grab and keep the essence of proper preparation before marriage.

Good marriages do not just happen, they are made to happen. A lot of it depends on the foundation that is laid. A good foundation would see a prosperous and formidable marriage in fulfilment. I believe that marriage should start from somewhere before the marriage proper.

It is rife for people begin relationships and back out along the way. Questions are: Is male-female relationship a trial and error thing? Who should you enter a relationship with and at what time? These questions are handled in this book including the challenges that are likely to be faced in course of such relationships.

Relationships should end in marriage ultimately.

Therefore, one should be prepared well enough for all the challenges of relationship and have a motive of marriage at the end. In preparation you have to do a good self - examination to know your personality and usual temperament.

This among other things would give you an idea of whom you may want to live with for the rest of your life. Additionally, praying before going out to search for a partner helps a lot. It helps to avoid potentially bad relationships and draw the right person close in sharp perspective.

This book is a must read for all young people who want to enter into a relationship leading to marriage. Ideas in this book are drawn out of the experiences of my life and other people. "There is nothing new under the sun," draw from this rich experience and launch unto the path of a successful relationship. Buy one for a friend who is not in a relationship and another for one who is struggling in or trying to maintain a relationship.

God bless your heart as you read.

DEDICATION

I dedicate this book to all the youth in this world.
I pray that the good Lord leads you to your
rightful partner.

CHAPTER **ONE**

Acronym For Relationship

Every journey is undertaken to reach a destination. Nevertheless, without the needed preparation you can never reach your destination. Relationship is a life journey that needs maximum preparation lest you fail to reach the landing place. Many have failed this journey for various reasons (some because of physical beauty, others for financial support, pleasure, and sex among others.)

I know someone who went into a relationship with a lady he was 'discipling' with the motive of helping her grow in Christ. That is so absurd—that is why you need to take your time and make the right decision. I once went into a relationship with a young, handsome, and caring gentleman out of curiosity; he was so handsome I didn't want any other girl to have him.

Every individual begins a relationship with a

different motive; either for fun, the beauty of it,to satisfy their sexual desires, wealth. These reasons cited can't produce a lasting relationship, will fall apart soon.

The simplest definition for relationship per my understanding is the "state of connection or been connected". You don't begin a relationship with someone unless you are already connected to the person. You relate with your family because there is already a "blood connection"; you relate with your friends because of "common interest connection" as well as you relate with God due to "Spirit connection". Finally, you relate with boyfriend/girlfriend or husband /wife due to "purpose connection" therefore you need to discover the "agent of connection" before the relationship can start.

The question is "what connects you to that man/woman? If you realize that, what connects you and the person you have interest in is other than PURPOSE, then that cannot lead to marriage in a Godly function. The only connection that leads to being husband/wife is Purpose so before you even decide to begin a relationship that leads to marriage, you first need to know your purpose, your need to know the timing for your purpose and relationship- get your timing right.

Relationship is a journey to the land of marriage which involves commitment and responsibility. Therefore, not every guy/lady is qualified for this journey because some have made up their minds not to marry or not to commit to one lady/gentleman. In view of this, you have to be vigilant and careful in your choice of guy/lady to start this journey with. If you detect he/she is irresponsible and not committed, it's a sign of unpreparedness on their part, meaning he/she is in for the fun and not for the purpose of that journey.
Any guy/lady who is not ready to commit is unworthy of a relationship. Never entertain such people or else you will end up heart broken and time wasted! If they are not ready for a commitment, it is better for them to be single than be in a relationship and waste others time. It is even serious when a lady gives out her body to a guy who will use and later dump you.

Be vigilant, it's not anybody you should be in a relationship with. Accept the ones who are matured in wisdom& knowledge, responsible and committed, they can take you to the land of marriage!

For a relationship to stand the test of time, it must be built on a good motive. In view of this, an acronym for the word "relationship" will help you understand its journey well. The first letter for relationship is R, which stands for

- **RESPECT**

Respect is key in relationships, the basic element on which every relationship thrives. Without it, all the elements required for a successful relationship aren't important since a relationship cannot be forced to thrive without respect. From an architectural perspective, respect is likened to the foundation of a building, without the foundation (respect), there is no (strong) building (lasting relationship).

So many relationships have broken up due to lack of respect. Many young women and men in this contemporary world lack respect for the elderly, how much more their own mates! Familiarity they say breeds contempt. Respect your partner's privacy, know how to relate with them in public even in unusual cases when they do something to provoke you. Know how to ask things from them without getting them offended and in their absence, know how to speak of them.

It is so sad to see two lovers embarrassing themselves in public, exchanging unpleasant words, sometimes resulting into a fight. Regardless of one's family background, you need to show respect if you desire to be in a serious relationship. Respect your partner (don't fake it), and it will surely be reciprocated.

Respect means recognizing your own worthand the worth of others. When we respect our partner, we are able to avoid pettiness, jealousy and cruelty. Respecting your partner as well as yourself enables you to build strong and long lasting relationship.

EXAMINATION

Examination here refers to self-examination, the study of one's own behaviour and motivation. The ability to know yourself is very important as it propels you into knowing and accepting the right people in your life. You need to examine yourself thoroughly, find out what you like, dislike, the type of man or woman you want, what you are able to do naturally. Are you quick tempered, loving, caring and tolerant? You cannot expect to know your partner if you lack in depth knowledge of who you are.

For example, what are the things that motivates you? By knowing this, you will be well equipped to find someone who stirs up your motivation, who pushes you to achieve greater things, enhancing a successful relationship leading to marriage.

You need to know all these things about yourself before getting into a relationship. In the next chapter, I will delve deeper into self-examination. Knowing yourself helps you to choose the right partner.

- **LOVE**

This is one of the most vital virtues you need before entering into a relationship. Most people have unrealistic expectations from their partners, this is because they do not understand what love is. You need to understand what love really is, in that way, you will know when someone really loves you. After you have acquired much knowledge about love, then you need to love yourself, appreciate who you are, whether short, tall, fat, slim, dark or fair. After loving yourself, then you prepare to love the person who comes into your life genuinely without compromising on your values. Most women are victim in compromising their values in a relationship, this is not a healthy thing to do. Let the man accept you for who you are and love you not because of something he is getting from you.

- **ADMIRATION**

When you admire a person, you never lose interest in them. Admiration is respecting and having a warm approval for someone or a thing. Admire every good thing your partner does; don't be jealous if they progress more than you. Support them because the moment you begin to get jealous of your partner's achievements, you put an end to the relationship.

■ TRUST

I love the song, 'Trust and obey, for there is no other way...' The best way to be happy and full of joy is to trust yourself and your partner. However, before trusting him or her, you have to make sure that you are truly trustworthy. If you are not a trustworthy person, when you enter into a relationship, you will always suspect your partner of cheating or hiding something from you.

■ IMPERVIOUS

If you are easily agitated, hurt, annoyed, and always nag, you need to change before you enter a relationship. Be impervious, not easily influenced by a feeling or argument because it will help anytime a misunderstanding arises since you'll know how to calm your partner's temper.

■ OVERCOMER

A person who always overcomes difficult situations never gives up easily in life as well as in relationships. Be an overcomer in your life and relationship—this will make the relationship last since you won't easily give up but fight to the end.

- **NURTURE**

Proverbs 22: 6 says "Train up the child the way he should go so when he grows he will not depart from it" Even a relationship with the great potential of success needs to be nurtured. Nurturing makes the relationship new and fresh every passing day. Spice it up with what you've got, make it grow and be new. Nurture it with love, care, trust, admiration, and respect.

- **SINCERITY**

Practise sincerity if you are not a sincere person. Be sincere to yourself no matter what the situation may be. Always speak the truth; let truth be your hallmark every day even if saying the truth will lead to another mess because truth is like a surgery; it hurts but heals. A lie is like a painkiller, gives instant relief but has side effects.

- **HONESTY**

Be honest in your dealings with people because honesty has led people to become great men and women in the world. Some people you meet will test your honesty before dealing with you so applying that into a relationship will help you mature and lead you to great places.

- **INVESTIGATION**

To investigate means to make a detailed inquiry or systematic examination. An investigation is done to reveal deep secrets or hidden things. Before getting into a relationship, one has to investigate the person whom he/she is about to go out with. Dig into his or her family background and personal life: friends, career, religion (Christian or not), among others. All these factors are needed in a relationship so make sure you do a thorough investigation.

Lastly, the last letter of relationship, P, means:

- **PATIENCE**

In Asante Twi, we say, "Aboterewienkunimdie," which means that patience calms many stormy situations, breaks mountains into valleys and covers up valleys to become a mere ground. Be patient in whatever you do in this life for success can be achieved through patience and a relationship can lead to marriage through patience.

CHAPTER TWO

Self- Examination

Life is sometimes hard as stone and unpleasant like vomit, so is marriage likened to itbut you still have to make it to the top. Marriage is a journey, if you are oblivious of your destination whiles in a relationship, then the right step and decision must be made —to quit or to know its destination.

Well, before embarking on a journey, certain preparations are made but my question is"What do you need or take alongwhen embarking on a journey? Don't be confused, the answer lies here;

- **THE CAR**

Every journey undertaken needs a vehicle either by air, land or sea no matter its distance, whether short or long. With regards to marriage, due to its long distance, one has to be fully prepared before embarking on such journey since you can get stacked in the middle of the journey when careful preparation is not made. The journey to marriage is likened to a journey on land, which can either be smooth as a velvet or rough as a badger's arse.

In relation to a journey on land, the first required vehicle is a car. The car represents the traveller's body, whether he/she is physically, mentally, spiritually, financially and emotionally matured to start the journey of marriage. Marriage requires maturity in every facet of your life therefore one has to fully scan him/herself to make sure his/her emotions, finance, spiritual, physical and mental being is stable.

Therefore, deciding to start this big step of relationship which will lead to marriage, one has to be fully prepared; gain in-depth knowledge through books, seminars and also, work hard to flood every unwanted baggagewhich can destroy the relationship.

Another important requirement for this journey is a strong, good engine since a car with a faulty engine can travel as slow as a tortoise and might not be able to get to its destination.

- **THE STRONG ENGINE**

Anytime I visit car dealers, one common but important question most buyers ask 'Is the engine strong?" Every car needs a strong engine, no matter how beautiful the car is, the engine determines its functionality whether it will last long and can travel fast or not. The strong engine symbolizes your heart. The issues of life lies in your heart, due to this, a heart that is soft, easily hurt,and full of mistrust, dishonesty and can't endure pain shouldn't be used for this kind of journey for it doesrequires a strong heart; full of compassion, love, patience, trust, tolerance and endurance.

People change with time, it doesn't happen in a blink of an eye therefore you need capacity to tolerate the things, attitudes and behaviours you dislike as you wait patiently for change. If you can't do this, then you are not ready for a long lasting relationship leading a committed marriage. You must train your heart to be strong; to learn how to overlook and ignore certain attitudes, when to speak and the moment to be silent.

Most relationships and marriages have become bitter as gall and black as coal due to issues of the heart. A long-lasting relationship leading to a committed marriage needs a strong heart, invest time to build yourself for this journey. Work on your heart; if you are quick tempered, easily agitated and not tolerant, learn how to channel these negative energies into positive ones.

I used to be quick tempered, would quickly react and later regret so I decided to leave the scene of action anytime something or someone infuriated me. I would take a walk, talk to myself and always felt refreshed when I returned. That's the perfect moment I could settle the issue but in the heat of the moment, you would just worsened it.

There are a lot of things you can do instantly when angry to avoid pettiness; either take a walk, sleep or find something which requires energy to do. When the atmosphere is as clear as crystal, you can solve the problem at hand. Your heart is very important for this journey.

There are some attitudes and hidden things you can never see through the course of the relationship, but begins to manifest during the marriage. If your heart is not strong to tolerate and to find means to deal with it, you might get frustrated. It takes only a spiritual eye to see beyond the facade. Marriage is a long journey; one needs a strong engine (heart), very enduring and easy to adapt to all kinds of roads (character) before starting it. Once you've acquired the car and fixed the strong engine, you need fuel to enable the car to move.

- **THE FUEL**

A car without a fuel is like a dead goat, it can't be eaten becoming useless. The car becomes static and immobile, no use for it. Fuel enables a car to travel to any distance but it can go very far dependent on how much fuel bought. Fuel used here refers to a job. One cannot marry without being employed or else you become a burden to your partner. Marrying without a job or something to lean on financially is like a dried sea; all the fishes will die, you can't actually survive.

Most couples who depended on the love they had for each other to marry irrespective of no job and money thinking they could survive, I can boldly say such marriages have fallen apart if they still lived in that condition. Even those who had jobs & money but some unexpected circumstances made them to lose their jobs and money, are trying to make the marriage work, it's definitely not easy to be in a marriage where there is financial instability. At least, get something doing that can raise money no matter how small it is.

There are different kinds of fuel: diesel, petrol, kerosene, charcoal and gas. The different kinds represent the individual intellects; some are educated and others are not but may have their own vocation. Educated working people can marry without having problems concerning provision and upkeep of the family.

Furthermore, those who have their own vocations,

such as hairdressers, fashion designers, mechanics, carpenters to mention but few, also do not have any problem at all. Remember, a job that can earn you money, which can actually grant you power to marry, cater for your wife and children is what is needed.

Just as a car needs fuel to move, so also a marriage requires a job to fuel it. Being on a long journey such as marriage requires much fuel; one can start the journey with the needed fuel (high paid job) or purchase some (small businesses) beforehand and buy more (becomes rich after marriage) as they move on. Meaning, some people are already rich before they get married, others are not but get to the level of richness after marriage.

After you've got your car, acquired your strong engine, and fuelled it, you need the master key because one key cannot match all cars; every car has its own key.

- **THE MASTER KEY**

A car becomes static and immobile without its rightful key to operate it. The rightful key, when inserted causes the car to operate so as every relationship leading to marriage needs a master key which can access any car. The master key signifies prayer. Prayer is the answer to every situation; without it, one cannot make it in life. In

1Thessalonians 5:17, it is written"pray without ceasing", because the moment you stop praying, your enemies gain advantage to destroy you.

You do not wrestle against flesh and blood, but principalities, rulers of darkness and their only antidote is Prayer. A prayerful woman/ man is able to resist the devil and live a glorious life, worthy of emulation. Prayers help and keep you in check as a Christian, never depart from it.

Prayers build up your spiritual being, leading you in making rightful decisions for this journey and exposing all hidden things unto you. In the book of Isaiah 62:6-7 and I quote, "O Jerusalem, I set upon your walls watchmen to guide you, do not keep silent those who call upon the name of the Lord for I have set my angels to hear whatever you say and establish it." Prayers concerning your marriage should not be toyed with.

Pray until the Lord hears and establishes you. God reveals himself to you anytime you pray and He even directs your path, for His word says in Proverbs 3:5-6, "Trust in the Lord with all your heart, lean not unto your own understanding; in all thy ways acknowledge Him and He shall direct thy paths."

Trusting God through prayers will open many

closed doors to you. Sometimes, when the men or women around you are many and you have to choose among the lot, it's easy to make a wrong decision if you are not careful. At such a time, you need to pray fervently for God's guidance and direction.

Start your car with the master key so that when those who use other keys fail, you'll rather triumph for your key worked and succeeded above all the ordinary keys.

After acquiring the master key, you need to check the tyres, whether they are hard or flat.

■ THE TYRES

Every car has tyres just as every marriage involves a man and a woman. The tyres hold the car; without it, the car cannot move. Without a man or woman, there cannot be marriage. One needs someone in his/her life before starting this journey. Now, this is what a woman and a man trying to get into relationship that would lead to marriage can assess:

■ THE FIRST TYRE (MAN)

This is the most critical stage when a person is ready to embark on the journey to marriage. Remember, a flat tyre can't take you far. If you are a responsible man, you need a visionary woman to embark on this journey. This moment is very crucial; the man needs to be very careful and vigilant. A visionary woman is one who fears the Lord as Proverbs 31:30 says, "Favour is deceitful, and beauty is vain: but a woman that fears the Lord, she shall be praised."

You need to ask yourself so many questions, "Does the qualities the woman exhibits the ones you desire? Does she respect people? Is she a Christian or not? If she's a Christian, does she fear God? What can she do naturally? Can she cook well? Is she a family woman who can manage the home and take care of the children? Can you reason with her always in matters that bothers you? Can she give you peace? All these questions must have answers.

Moreover, a visionary woman lives a life of excellence, has integrity and being her best in everything. She is unique, doesn't need a man to feel complete and whole but knows a man from the Lord is a blessing. You need a lady who is committed, honest and trustworthy. You have to cross-examine her very well; the way she speaks, how she reacts when she's angry, disturbed, hurt, among others. Also, how does she dress? Is it decent or not? Find out her educational level and the family to which she belongs. Most of all, do you love her genuinely or is it just her beauty that attracts you to her.

A woman who fears the Lord is always calm, sincere, honest, faithful, patient, loves praying, studying the Bible and is hardworking—men, watch out for such women. As a woman is a **HELP-MEET**, you must make sure the woman's vision is in line with your purpose so that both of you can fulfil destiny. Relationship is not only about two people been in love but about purpose and the fulfilment of destiny. Take notice of this as you seek the face of the Lord for a woman.

NB: You won't get all these qualities in a woman, you will notice some and as you embark on the relationship, you cultivate her to bring out the rest. She can have 50% initially but as you progress, you will discover her more, either good or bad depending on how you treat her too.

▪ THE SECOND TYRE (WOMAN)

As a woman, you also need a man of value and in whose purpose lays your vision. Remember it's not advisable to base your selection of a man on only physical qualities—that is dangerous. According to Plato, a Greek political thinker, there are three qualities competing in the human soul-**REASON,** the ability to think and make great decisions; **APPETITIVE,** one's desires to eat, drink, have sex and learn; and **SPIRITED**, which talks about one's anger, courage, tameness, shyness, among others. He asserts that a man can be Just if the appetitive and spirited submit to the reason always. If you are someone who always loves eating, sex, and partying, then your appetitive quality is above the reason and spirited. When it comes to a relationship, one has to put reason above the other qualities. Don't allow the man's physique only to attract you, but his inner qualities too-responsible, goal-getter, disciplined, gentle, honest, loving, humble, and respectful.

In addition, check the way he speaks: Does he talk about the future? Does he include you anytime he talks about the future? How does he relate to his family members, especially the women? Is he hardworking or lazy? Is he a family man? Can he provide spiritually, emotionally, financially for you and the family? Is he matured enough to be a husband and father?

Moreover, a faithful and Godly man will lead you in your walk with God, protect your purity and will show you why God didn't want you settle with past guys if there were any. A man whowill lead you to achieve your goals too, very understanding and supportive.

I want you to remember this always: Boys build shacks but men build homes, so watchout. Get a man who fears God because they always act with diligence, make their wives happy, hate to cheat and do not mingle or spend a lot of time with friends. They always profess their love for their wives to the people close to them.

Women, watch out for such men for they are the best tyres to use for this journey.

NB: He will possess some of these qualities but as you progress, more will be revealed; depending on how you treat him too.

Now that the tyre has been fixed, the journey must begin; however, there is one thing you need to know before you start the journey. Sometimes, we make so many mistakes because of this thing I'm about to introduce to you— the spare tyre.

THE SPARE TYRE
The spare tyre used here is not another man/woman, but your emotions. One needs to set his or her emotions right so that if the tyre accidentally bursts (a break-up), you can handle it with ease. Some people lose their minds, sense of humour, and others even get to the extent of

becoming mentally retarded due to a break-up. It's not easy to handle a burst tyre (break-up) since it can land you into an accident (broken heart)—that's why one needs to set his or her emotions right and prepare for any misfortune.

Thus, when the unfortunate happens, even though it hurts, you can handle it very well without getting crushed. I'm sure you know that there have been cases where some car tyres burst (break-up) without leading to an accident (broken heart). You can also handle break ups well without your life being shattered.

CHAPTER **THREE**

Whiles In A Relationship

I'm supposing from the previous **CHAPTER**, you might have found the person who compliments your God-given purpose. From this point, a relationship is needed because the two of you have to connect. How do the two connect whiles in a relationship? When you read the bible Amos3:3 it says "can two walk together unless they agree". So, before the two can really connect, there has to be **AGREEMENT** on every issue relating to marriage and marital life as well as purpose and destiny.

For example; couples who don't attend the same church, it's dangerous sometimes because you are been fed with different teachings, a time will come one will think his/her church is better than the other leading to the unexpected. Also, a wife who is interested in family ceremonies and a husband who is not interested in that, these couples can face the unexpected if they don't find a way to agree on how such things should be avoided or compromised. With these examples, partners journeying towards marriage should take note and try to make agreement on all issues without affecting the other negatively.

Moreover, there has to be **EFFECTIVE COMMUNICATION,** where the two can be free to share everything including interests, goals and aspirations in life. Note this; it shouldn't always be romantic chat but life communication/ purpose communication. When communication is done well, it creates the environment of trust, belonging and companionship. It's a point where everything relating to the individual can be discussed; weakness, strengths, past and present. Examples are Abraham& Sarah, Isaac& Rebecca, Joseph& Mary in the bible, they really communicated. Likewise, if your relationship with God can be strong, it depends on communication to create a strong bond.

Now, after communication, you two need **FELLOWSHIP**. Is quite different from communication; it moves further to involve the two of you embarking on a similar course. Fellow means two or more people on a particular course and the ship means a travelling machine so fellowship is, partners embarking on a common agenda or purpose together. Your fellowship can be seen by engaging in something Godly together and it has to be sacred. It strengthens bond and affection.

Whiles in a relationship, **ATTRACTION** must work too. Attraction is something that pulls two or more things together therefore for the relationship to be stronger; there is the need for something that attracts you two together. Attraction can be physical, social or spiritual but as believers you don't build your attraction only on the physical because it's temporal; you need to build your attraction on something that is permanent or spiritual.

For instance, you don't date a lady/guy because he/she is beautiful or handsome, what if he/she grows old or gets an accident that disfigures him/her, will you still be attracted to him/her? I don't think so!! But if your attraction is on purpose which is spiritual, no matter what happens, you two would still be together because you might not find someone who can replace that attraction. Physical appearance is not enough; there should be something extraordinary; it could be character, spiritual gifts, purpose or something more permanent.

INTIMACY has been a controversial point when it comes to relationship because people don't know at which level to go in showing intimacy. What then is intimacy? Per my understanding, intimacy is togetherness, affirmation, rapport, attachment, familiarity, close association, and close relationship/understanding the two partners feel. Intimacy in this 21st century has all been based on sexual relationship. It is part in marriage but in the confines of relationship that leads to marriage, it has to be omitted. There are still more ways to show intimacy, per the definition, a person can show intimacy like understanding the other feelings and emotional complexities. It shouldn't always have to be sex; going to the beach, cinemas, window shopping to mention but few can all be means to show intimacy other than sex as believers.

LOVE LANGUAGE

Is there something called love language? Do we have a language lover's use? What makes you moved or attracted more to your partner? Well, after a few research, I discovered some school of thoughts have this notion that, there is indeed love languages partners use which draws them more close to one another. You might be wondering what these love languages are? It's not something strange or new, you can even guess right now before I lay them down. Since you are still guessing and can't fetch the right answers, let me help you. These love languages are touch, gifts, quality time, and communication and lastly, service.

According to this school of thoughts, when the two lovebirds understand each other's love language, they can be very intimate together.

Firstly, touch is a love language according to them and denotes that some people are moved by it but in this context of relationship that leads to marriage as a believer, you have to know your level of intimacy with your partner. I know as a believer in a relationship, the highest touch should be **HUG!** Anything extra should be possibly or forcibly prevented to avoid any immoral sexual intercourse. The ways to express intimacy in this love language is been a shoulder for the person to cry on, always holding your partners hand for her to feel protected, hugging your lover as an encouragement and a motivation but the lines have to be respected. Most ladies are in this category with a few guys.

The second love language is gifts. You see your ability to buy gifts for your partner is one of the ways to show intimacy to the people you love and care. They see gifts as precious things coming from a precious heart so, if you don't buy them gifts, it means you don't love them. Most at times, the people in this category are not looking for huge/expensive gifts; they are just looking for a little thing that tells them you still care about them. Those who are always looking for expensive gifts and disregard the little things are not in this category, therefore beware of them for they have ulterior motives, they really don't love you.

The next love language is quality time. With this category, it has both males and females. One way of expressing your love according to this school of thoughts is to have quality time with your partner thus move away from other relations and unnecessary commitments to spend time with your partner or fiancé. The two of you can visit interesting sites together, play a game, watch movies, go for concerts, eat together at restaurants to mention but few. Relationship that leads to marriage should not be that boring; there has to be something that keeps it running and that is intimacy.

Moreover, communication as a love language is one of the best tools to tighten bonds. Communication is one best tool to express intimacy; it should not be one-sided, one person willing to communicate all the time, rather both sides.

Finally, service is the last out of the five love languages, and most of the people that have their love language to be service are males. Some say your ability to serve them shows love, a personthat can really serve appeals to his/her heart. An example is when my friend Kay who was in a relationship with two ladies had an accident but Jenny more than 400km from Kay came all the way to serve him; dressed his wound and took proper care of him. Meanwhile, Janet who was quite closer to Kay didn't bother to take care of him but bought him an expensive gift to wish him speedy recovery.

Because of this, Kay grew more found of Jenny and began to love her more than Janet. In the end, Kay married Jenny and now they are happily married with two kids; boy and girl. This is one of the many examples I have witnessed and runs in the world, most guys love ladies that are willing to serve them and not those who are willing to spend.

CHAPTER FOUR

Journey On A Tarred Road

When I was a child, my mum always preferred traveling to Accra than our hometown because she said the road to Accra was tarred, unlike the route to our hometown. I would laugh whenever she said that but little did I know she was speaking in proverbs.

After my senior high education, I decided to travel to Accra to experience for myself. During the journey, the road was so smooth, making it cool and exciting. I enjoyed the journey because I felt so comfortable, relaxed and happy when we got to Accra.

Although there were a few potholes, that did not disrupt the journey at all. Relationship can be likened to this journey. When your relationship is journeyed on a tarred road, there is comfort, relaxation, happiness, joy, love, protection, security and excitement.

As I said earlier, though there were few potholes, my journey was not destroyed. This could be likened to times when misunderstandings (potholes) could arise in a relationship, yet it cannot destroy it. When you begin the journey (relationship) on a smooth road, you can easily dodge the potholes (misunderstandings) or fall into it and move on again.

What this means is that, when misunderstanding occurs, some people easily solve it without turning into a big problem. The offender quickly accepts his/her mistake, apologizes (dodges the pothole) and makes amends (moves onto the smooth road again).

In relationships, others also wait for the potholes to be filled up by others before they move out of it. Some elders, pastors and friends come in to help resolve these matters (fill up the pothole) before they start afresh again (move onto the tarred road). Relationship journeyed on a tarred road leads to the following:

- **COMFORT**
I felt comfortable during my journey because the car moved so fast without stopping—the road was good which ensured a comfortable journey. This means that a relationship journeyed on a smooth road will go far without breaking up and eventually lead to marriage.

A comfortable relationship is one where you feel loved by your partner and there isn't the need to worry about your partner cheating. Being comfortable brings about relaxation since you don't have to check your partner's phone, diaries and other private stuff to ensure he or she is not cheating. You don't waste your time and energy on the wrong things; all you do is to move smoothly on the journey because you are sure that the car won't break down on the way.

- **HAPPINESS**

Reaching your destination brings about joy and happiness. Getting married to the right man or woman brings about so much happiness since your needs, whether sexual, emotional, physical and spiritual, are always satisfied. A journey made on a tarred road leads you safely to your destination; therefore, a relationship journeyed on smooth road leads you to marriage. Marrying the right man or woman will make your journey fulfilled and bring you joy and happiness.

- **PROTECTION**

There is protection in your relationship since God protects you and watches over your relationship. As you pray every day, committing your life and the journey you are on unto Him, he makes sure that nobody (including the enemy) comes to destroy it. For His word says in Ephesians 6:12 that we do not wrestle against flesh and blood but against principalities, evil doers, workers of iniquity, so He shall surely protect you from such wicked people and forces.

■ SECURITY

Just as the driver feels secure when he is on a road that is unlikely to give him any problems, so also people in relationships feel secure about each other and the journey they are on. When one has confidence in his or her partner, there is security and they need not worry about thieves (another man or woman) invading their house (relationship) and stealing their belongings (husband or wife to be).

When all these needs are met, the journey to marriage becomes enjoyable and trouble-free and it ends successfully (marriage).

CHAPTER **FIVE**

Journey On Untarred Road

Immediately I returned from Accra, I planned to visit my hometown, Sakora-Wonoo, for the first time in my life. As the journey begun, I realized why my mum was always unhappy about travelling to the village. Journeys made on untarred roads are very terrifying—full of pain, fear, and anxiety.

As the bus journeyed on the road, it began to shake vibrantly and intensively because the road was covered with gravels, very dusty and potholed.

■ POT-HOLES

The first obstacle I encountered was potholes. Potholes here refer to misunderstandings that arise in relationships. All over the world, relationships that were geared towards marriage have broken up due to misunderstandings. Almost all relationships, eventually, will run into potholes. Remember, potholes occur on the road when there is constant and excessive rainfall or flooding.

When it rains heavily and continuously for about a year, it wears down the road creating potholes—this also occurs in relationships. When two people in a relationship continuously argue or pick fights with each other, the relationship becomes potholed. A relationship whereby the man or woman did not take their time to know each other always leads to misunderstandings. Before starting a relationship, you must first be friends, gradually learn to respect each other's opinions and lastly, recognize the person's negative sides.

Partners do not wait patiently to get to know each other, when a person's negative attitude shows up, the other does not take it lightly and leads to misunderstandings. These misunderstandings can last a day, weeks, months and even years and soon, it becomes difficult for the relationship to be sweet, lovely, joyful and as happy as it used to be.

A relationship journeyed on potholes leads to discomfort, tiredness, and displeasure. A friend of mine, Abigail, courted a man called Anderson. Both families knew of their intentions and were studying each other. One day, Abigail complained bitterly about her man cheating on her. I asked how she had come up with such an idea. The only thing she could say was "she took his phone and he had saved someone's name as 'sweety.'

I couldn't help but laugh. She got angry and left without listening to what I had to say. The next day she called and said, she had followed her man when he was going out and surprisingly, she saw him get out of the taxi he had boarded to join another woman in a private car.

I told her to confront him whenever he paid her a visit. She didn't take my advice; rather, she decided to pay him back in his own coin. She accepted to go out with a man who had been pestering her for so long and eventually they went out on a date. Unluckily for her, she ended up in bed with him.

Two days later, her man visited and wanted to touch her, but she ignored him. She felt very uneasy about what she had done. She decided to confront him about the name he had saved on his phone as 'sweety.' He laughed and then explained that she was a friend who was helping him with an investment concerning a house that he was buying. Abigail did not believe him; Anderson dialled her digits and put the phone on loudspeaker so that Abigail could listen to their conversation. The man she had cheated on her partner with unexpectedlyshowed up at her residence the next day, calling her "my love". Unfortunately, Anderson found out that his woman had cheated and that was the end of the relationship.

Please be cautious anytime you suspect your lover of anything.

▪ GRAVELLED ROAD

Aside the pothole, the road was covered with gravels. These gravels on the untarred road symbolize pain in relationship. Travelling on gravels has an adverse effect on the tyres (couples), causing them to make noise, shaking and disturbing (arguments and strife) as the journey progresses.

The man or woman makes arguments that result in quarrels, especially on issues that are trivial. These quarrels cause so much pain and sadden the hearts of the couples.

Also, when you travel on a gravelled and dusty road, your hair, clothes and other belongings become dirty—the same applies to relationships. Everything you do becomes unpleasant, ugly, and unwelcomed in the eyes of your partner; anything concerning you becomes unattractive to your partner. Pain in one's heart can cause so many tragedies that may not be pleasant.

Another thing I encountered on the untarred road was

THE SHAKING OF THE CAR

Since the road was rough, gravelled and dusty, the car shook throughout the journey. There were times when some of the passengers actually fell off their seats—the road was so bad. Relationships also reach its shaky moment. When one offends the other, instead of apologizing and letting sleeping dogs lie, he or she feels too proud to do so. This makes them be at each other's nerves, causing their love, care, and affection for each other to be destroyed, leading to a break-up. Anything one partner does, begins to infuriate the other, which stirs up anger, hatred, and dispute among them.

A shaky car can fall easily just as a shaky relationship can easily break up, causing pain, sadness and sorrow. Just a little push (misunderstanding) can make it fall, so be careful when your journey reaches a shaky stage.

CHAPTER SIX

How To Move From An Untarred To A Tarred Road

If you get tired of being on the untarred road and you decide to go back onto the tarred one, these decisions can help you to enjoy your comfortable, relaxing and exciting journey of relationship again.

- **PRAY FERVENTLY**

To move from an untarred road to a tarred one, you have to fill the pothole, which refers to misunderstandings in relationships. The first thing to do when filling a pothole is to get some gravels, sand, cement, linking this in solving a misunderstanding in any relationship, you need to pray fervently and its ingredients are your Bible, faith and hope.

After studying the Bible, you must meditate upon the words, believing in whatever has been said and hoping that whatever you need shall be provided through your prayer. The book of Mark 11:24 says, "Therefore I say to you, what things so ever ye desire, when ye pray, believe that ye receive them and ye shall have them."

Communicate with God through prayers, telling him all that you are going through in the relationship, and He shall restore everything as it used to be. Don't stop praying, for the Bible says that the effectual fervent prayer of the righteous man avails much power (James 5:16). Prayer is the master key—use it well and you would never ever regret it.

- **TRUST GOD AND YOUR PARTNER**

Before filling the pothole, you got some ingredients such as sand, cement and gravels. Now, you need to add water to those ingredients. The water symbolises trust in a relationship. After praying about your relationship, develop a different kind of trust towards your partner. Mix prayers with trust because without trust, it will be difficult for the relationship to be sustained.

Trust is one of the most important foundations in building a relationship. Without it, the relationship that appears to be standing firm will just be blown away (break up) with a little wind (doubt). Always build your relationship with trust and it will go a long way for you.

Proverbs3:5 says, "Trust in the Lord with all your heart and lean not unto your own understanding." Trust God for a turnaround in your relationship for God alone can be trusted in such situations.

The moment you begin to have doubts about your

partner, confront him or her for an explanation before drawing conclusions. Don't always listen to what people tell you; at times, they may be against your relationship or may have feelings for your partner, so be vigilant and very careful of rumours.

- **LOVE UNCONDITIONALLY**

After mixing the ingredients with water, you have now come to the point of filling up the pothole. The best way to fill up a pothole is by gently pouring the concrete into the hole—this stands for love. Love gently and unconditionally. When you pour out prayers, trust in your partner and love unconditionally, your relationship will be filled to capacity.

Love is very important when solving issues of misunderstandings. Don't love selfishly, always expecting something in return. Don't always be at the receiving end of love—give yours out also. 1 John 3:18 talks about not loving in word or in tongue, but in deed and in truth. Some people always profess love to their partners, but their actions are contrary to what they say. Start loving in truth and deed, for that's the best way to express your love to your partner.

1 John 4:18 says, "There is no fear in love. But perfect love drives out fear, because fear has to do with punishment. The one who fears is not made perfect in love" (NIV). The moment you begin to

love without fear or insecurities, not thinking of your partner betraying, disappointing and dumping you, you love freely and unconditionally. Such love ensures a smooth journey to marriage because there is no time for insecurities or fear that your partner may hurt you.

Love is patient; it never gives up. It makes the hard heart tender, refreshes the mind, endures pain, forgives and forgets. Love gives meaning to one's life—it energizes the weak heart. Love gives you the power to fight and break all the odds that you encounter. Love makes you feel relaxed and happy always.

- **BE HUMBLE**

After praying, trusting God and your partner, and showing your unconditional love, the next thing to do is to show humility. Showing humility and love during a misunderstanding is vital. Humility makes an angry spirit calm because when you are humble, your words are always refreshing.

James 4:10 talks about humbling ourselves in the sight of the Lord, and He shall lift us up. Humbling yourself in the sight of God and your partner makes them love, cherishyou and you begin to feel blessed and loved.

Be humble in the way you talk, address issues, and confront arguments, quarrels, and misunderstandings in your relationship. Humility can take you far and as such, it must not be taken for granted. Humility is a habit that must be practised always in order for it to become a character.

Learn to be humble for humility goes with obedience and submissiveness. Being humble requires you to be obedient and submit to your partner.

- **SET A GOAL**

A suffered- relationship need not happen again so what you've got to do is set a goal this time. Don't repeat the same standards you used therefore setting a goal will help make things right and special. Now, make it a point to set a goal every month which should be achievable- involve your partner so as to know what he/she wishes to do that month.

This will help you know how far the relationship can go and what you both can do. Also, write down those you couldn't achieve and make an effort to find ways to deal with it. Don't set goals that are too difficult for both of you to accomplish- it should be simple. Always involve your partner so as to know his/her schedules, what he/she is interested in doing that month and how you going to organise your activities.

Setting a goal in a relationship makes everything organised and planned; you don't waste time and resources on unnecessary things and that makes the relationship grow each and every day since everything done is planned and new things are achieved every month. Note this, let your goal be all round, not always emphasizing on one thing. Let it cover all aspects of life; prayers, fasting, outing, church, parties, educational tour, window shopping and among others.

Remember you are building the relationship on the goals you set so if it's always about chilling, it wouldn't be effective: let it be concise, interesting, informative and educative. You can set a day out to educate yourselves; to learn new things and add it to the ones you know. Be always objective in the goal, let it spice the relationship and not make it dull or boring.

I know some people have not practiced this before but I can say it works very much. There are some times you feel like not doing anything and even your partner becoming too boring for you- the old chats, messages, moves among others which makes you bored sometimes. Setting a goal every month will prevent this boredom since new things are been done and shall surely spice up the relationship.

CHAPTER SEVEN

The Resting Point

Anytime you travel, you may make a stop, have a snack, relieve yourself, relax or walk for a while. This break is very important; without it, the journey will be very tiring and stressful. Some people may not get to the rest stop due to an accident—a break-up in terms of relationships. The rest stop is a place where you feel relaxed because you are 80% sure that you will reach your destination. This place determines whether you'll make it through the journey or not. The relationship journey also needs a resting place, if not it cannot reach its destination.

This resting point is **COUNSELLING.** Before two people can get married, they need to go through counselling, which is usually done in the church by the marriage counselling committee made up of elders of the church. A date is then fixed for couples who want to get married so that they can be counselled.

During counselling, questions are asked and important topics concerning marriage are discussed. Sometimes, both partners go together; at times, they go separately. Partners are asked to write down the likes and dislikes of the other. Then, the counsellors compare their responses in order to find out if the couple are compatible or not and to find out how much they know about each other. They also try to find out if they are both ready to marry or not through the questions they ask.

Counsellors usually set up a group to investigate secretly into the families of the partners, their family behaviour, attitudes, and religion to mention but few. They also find out if the man is financially, emotionally, spiritually and physically ready to get married. The investigators also find out if the woman is ready to be a wife—how she keeps the home, if she is disciplined, hardworking, respectful, peaceful, reasonable, and how she relates to her family. The counsellors make sure that the woman's attitude towards people in and outside her family is encouraging and welcoming. All these investigations are done thoroughly to ensure a good marriage.

The couple are then asked individually to write their expectations of their marriage. The counsellors also ask them to check their genotype, blood group, and test their HIV status. All these are done to ensure a healthy marriage. Sometimes, after going through all these, the counsellors may advise them to take time to study each other or break up, if they foresee any potential problems. If you do not follow the counsellor's advice, the church will not bless your marriage.

The counsellors are experienced people and stand on behalf of God to show you the best way to marriage, but it's not always their judgement are right. You can't skip counselling so be ready for it as you journey on the road to marriage. Be prepared, for many questions will be asked. If you don't know your partner well, it is time for you to study him or her.

CHAPTER **EIGHT**

Reaching The First Destination

Anytime you travel, although you have one main destination, you go through a few short destinations before you reach the ultimate one. The moment you get off the bus, you may board one or two taxis before you reach home (the ultimate destination). Such also happens in relationships. After counselling, the next destination is the setting of the date and preparations for the marriage.

The first destination is the setting of the date for the marriage. Setting the date signifies the union you are about to have and that everlasting life you are going to share. Some people don't know the meaning of the date they set but I don't blame them. People are usually in a haste to get married; therefore they don't understand the preparations they make.

Here is an acronym for the **DATE** you set for your marriage. The **'D'** stands for:

- **DETERMINATION**

From the Collins Pocket Dictionary, determination means "firmly decided, unable to be dissuaded." This means that you must make up your mind that no matter what happens, you'll stick to your partner without been dissuaded by the situation or pressures around. You have decided to be with your partner forever and to spend your entire life with him or her.

Anytime you set a date for your marriage, remember that you have made a firm decision to spend your entire life with your partner, so determine that no matter what comes your way, you shall be there for each other. If you are determined to excel in life, you break all the odds, obstacles and challenges to achieve what you've wished for; let this be your attitude also in marriage.

You have to break all the odds, obstacles and challenges that come your way to be able to stick to each other; if not, you will be easily persuaded and influenced by others to break the spirit of determination. Always be determined, not easily influenced by situations or people around.

Determination leads to success therefore if you are truly determined, your marriage will go a long way despite all the challenges and obstacles. Always remember that the date is also part of the marriage since it actually seals the deal.

The **'A'** stands for:

- **ASSURANCE**

Assurance is a state of mind in which one is free from doubt. If you assure somebody of something, you make a commitment to do (or not to do) something in the future. When the date is set for the marriage ceremony, it brings assurance to both partners. It makes both parties aware of the marriage they are about to enter. Once the date is set, it shows that both partners are convinced that they can make it through the marriage and that they are meant for each other.

When someone assures you of something, the person makes a promise to do something. In a marriage, both partners assure each other of their love and promise to stay true to each other. Assurance binds people together because they have made a commitment to each other. It becomes difficult to be separated since they make a promise to love and to cherish each other. The date marks the day when they actually profess their desire to undertake the journey of marriage. Hence, before entering into a marriage, let the 'date' speak for you.

Rest assured in God and your partner—do not allow anybody or any problem to tear you apart. In the date is the assurance, so always allow the 'date' to manifest itself in the marriage you are about to undertake.

The **'T'** in **DATE** stands for:

- **TRUTHFULNESS**

Being truthful is not easy for worldly people. However, it is your duty as a child of God to be truthful since your Father is a truthful God. Always be truthful no matter how hard the situation is. Marriages nurtured with truth always bring about happiness since there are no secrets kept from each other.

As you set the date, remember that you have made a promise to be truthful to each other even though the truth may hurt sometimes. Don't fill your heart with secrets, for someday it shall surely come out. Everything that is hidden can be found. Always be truthful, abounding in grace of the Almighty God. The Bible makes us understand that speaking the truth sets you free, clearing all guilt and heaviness in your mind and heart. Learn to speak the truth always, for it shall bring you happiness, joy, long life and prosperity.

The last letter **'E'** represents:

- **ENJOYMENT**

After determination, assurance and truthfulness, then comes enjoyment. Enjoy the marriage with love, care, respect for each other, and gentleness. Remember the 'date' seals the marriage, so now is the time for both of you to enjoy what you've waited so long for.

Marriage without enjoyment and happiness is

useless, hence make sure that the marriage you are about to enter brings you happiness, joy, love and fulfilment. Enjoy it to the fullest; withstand temptations, challenges, obstacles and all the odds associated with it.

Spark up your marriage, always trying something new to boost the love and happiness in your marriage. Do not let the marriage become stale—always try new ideas and actions to put a spark in your relationship. Find ways to make the marriage attractive to each other. Blend your love, care, respect and trust with the word of God for God is your stronghold, advisor and helper.

You now know what the 'date' stands for in marriage—determination, assurance, truthfulness and enjoyment.

CHAPTER NINE

Reaching The Final Destination

The final destination for every relationship is marriage. Every relationship that thrives on good motives always reaches the final destination, which is marriage. It has its issues as everything else does; however, God is more concerned about it.If beauty,fame and attraction bring ideal marriages, then celebrities will have the best marriages. Marriage goes beyond fame, beauty and attraction. If the foundation on which you started the relationship with is wrong, then your marriage won't stand the test of time.

Marriage is good and beautiful but it has a purpose. We don't just marry, if you can't love yourself, build your career and be complete about yourself, then you are not ready for marriage. Marriage is about two whole people who have come together to share companionship and to fulfil purpose together, not about fun, pleasure and dependency. The man's purpose must sync with his woman's vision, so both can accomplish one thing with satisfaction.

Marriage goes beyond finding a man or woman,putting the ring on and living in the same house. If it is like that then there wouldn't be divorce. It is about finding the one who meets your purpose, can help, support and bring it into reality. Since you are both accomplishing one purpose,it always brings satisfaction and fulfilment. No matter the quarrels and fights, purpose will still unite you two.

Marry for the right reasons and you will enjoy it forever,don't just marry anyone but the one who truly compliments you and share in your vision/purpose.

In Genesis 2:18 says, "Then the Lord God said, it is not good for the man to live alone, I will make a suitable companion to help him." Marriage is God's idea and He approves of it. Most people do not take their time when choosing their life partners, thus making mistakes, later regretting, and results in divorce which God hates.

In recent times, about 70% of marriages are dissolved in Ghana. I have always wondered what causes break-ups in marriage. Marriage is very essential and I cherish it so much because God has really touched my heart regarding it. If you get into a bad marriage, that's the end of your life because it slowly destroys your life as well as your future. This is why I first introduced you to the right route in reaching the perfect destination.

Marriage holds your life, future and everything of yours and as such, one needs to give it a lot of attention. Many of my family members have suffered bad marriages that is why I am so passionate about it. Before there can be a good marriage, there should be sacrifice, mutual understanding, consensus building, trust, love, and care.

Marriages require sacrifice; partners should be willing to make sacrifices for each other. To sacrifice is to give up something valuable in order to maintain a relationship. Sacrifice should be reciprocal in a marriage; one partner should not always be the one to benefit from sacrifices. The other partner should also be willing to sacrifice when necessary so that one person does not find him/herself being the only one making sacrifices. There are times in a relationship where one would offend the other due to their different characters, attitudes, and egos—this is the time you have to show your partner how much you cherish him or her. Such offences can be so painful and tough that you may think divorce is the best solution; however, you can opt not to break the marriage.

Marriage is not the same as an ordinary relationship in which you can just opt out when you get tired of the person. In marriage, there is nothing like that—you have to endure a lot of tough situations. A typical illustration is the story of Abraham and Sarah in the Bible. They went through a lot of hardship, but they were determined and trusted each other. They never thought of getting divorced when Sarah had still not conceived, but endured to the end.

Most couples can't endure marriage without children for even two years. They soon begin to look for opportunities to opt out. You have to know also that marriage goes beyond two people saying vows. I don't think couples realize that when you marry someone, you also marry that person's family. Having good relationships with the in-laws is important. Anyone who has had conflicts in that arena will tell you that bad relationships with in-laws can be a nightmare.

Every lasting marriage requires selfless love, grounded in truth, trust each other implicitly, unending commitment, mutual respect, mutual submission, willingness to learn and adjust to situations, faithfulness, financial stability, emotional stability and peace.

Every signs of future problems must be addressed, dealt with before the marriage, never rush when there are serious issues to be handled and dealt with. This final destination should bring joy, peace, happiness, fulfilment and not regret, sadness, conflicts to mention but few. Marriage should be sweet, not sour then being single would have been better than a sorrowful marriage. And this can achieved, when you take your time in making the right decisions.

According to Joni Lamb, Daystar Television Network's co-host of celebration, she said there are ten challenges in marriage which most couples find it difficult to deal with which are

- Putting God first in the marriage
- Managing money and financial pressures
- Communicating effectively and resolving conflict
- Being in agreement on how to raise children
- Putting your spouse before your children
- Dealing with addictions (drugs, alcohol, abuse, pornography)
- Maintaining a healthy sex life
- Learning to forgive one another
- Handling health issues
- Balancing schedules.

I can emphatically say that's very true and as such you need to take note of it.

CHAPTER **TEN**

What Ought To Be Done
Submissiveness

All married men expect their wives to be submissive in marriage therefore they have to also play their role very well in loving and cherishing them. Ephesians 5:21 says, "Wives and husbands, submit yourselves to one another because of your reverence for Christ." In this chapter, would focus on wives who are richer and better-looking than their husbands and feel that they do not need to be submissive because they can get anything they want on their own.

It's totally wrong for women to think that way. The book of Ephesians 5:22 and 24 says that wives should submit to their husbands as to the Lord. Wives must therefore submit completely to their husbands just as the Church submits to Christ. Submissiveness shouldn't be done out of force but out of love. It should be from the heart, naturally respecting your husband and following his lead as the church follows Jesus lead.

This error must be corrected to ensure a successful marriage, the fact that you are richer and beautiful than your husband doesn't give you the right to disrespect and walk on them. There should be mutual submission and a lot of adaptability. This ought to be done in marriage;

- **SELFLESS LOVE**

Love is patient, kind, forgiving, longsuffering, caring, gentle, enduring and welcoming. Love is very important in marriage; it conquers everything. God demonstrated His love towards us by allowing his ONLY begotten son Jesus Christ to come and die in other for us to be saved and to gain redemption. Married men and women ought also to love themselves unconditionally, putting aside their egos and pride.

To the men, Ephesians 5:25-33 says, "Husbands, love your wives just as Christ loved the church and gave His life for it. He did this to dedicate the church to God by His word, after making it clean by washing it in water, in order to present the church to Himself in all its beauty—pure and faultless, without spot or wrinkle or any other imperfection."

Therefore, men ought to love their wives just as they love their own bodies, helping them grow to overcome their weaknesses so they become blameless before them and others just Christ cleansed us from all sin. A man who loves his wife loves himself. (It is not normal for people to hate their own bodies; they feed them and take care of them, just as Christ does the church, for we are members of His body).

As the scripture says, "For this reason a man will leave his father and mother and unite with his wife; and the two will become one." There is a deep truth revealed in this scripture in addition to its meaning concerning Christ and the church—every husband must love his wife as himself.

Men usually do not show how much they love their wives or how they truly feel about them. They hide it within because they feel that if a woman knows how much you love her, she will take advantage of you. It's an unhealthy thing to do in a relationship.

Love is sharing. Love is not self-seeking. It never gives up even when the going becomes tough. It is not selfish, always wanting to excel higher than the other. Rather, love is about helping each other, complimenting and praising your lover always.

Love is long-suffering. Consider the love Jacob had for Rachel. He was willing to work an additional seven years just to be with her. You must learn to endure a lot if you truly love someone.

- **MUTUAL RESPECT**

Respect is very vital when it comes to marriage. Respect is the acknowledgement we extend to a person irrespective of the person's status, belief, among others. A marriage where there is mutual respect is very good, smooth and enjoyable. Both partners should respect each other's decisions; remember you are two different people getting to know and adapt to each other. Mutual respect is essential in maintaining a healthy relationship. A situation where one refuses to respect the other can result in big problem, thereby destroying the marriage.

Always be cautious of the kind of words you use, it should be harmless rather than harmful to the soul. "Pleasant words are like a honeycomb, Sweetness to the soul and health to the bones" (Proverbs 16:24). Respect each other's professions, talents, goals, decisions.

- **TOLERANCE**

Tolerance is the willingness to accept somebody or something, especially, opinions and behaviour that you may not agree with. Partners may not always fully agree with each other, but they must learn to accept and become tolerant of their differences. Tolerance is what you are willing to put up with or deal with for the rest of your married days. Sometimes, you have to be patient and try not to argue unnecessarily. I have formed acronyms with the word **'TOLERANCE'**.

T- Trust
O- Obey
L- Listen
E- Endure
R- Respect
A-　　 Assist
N- Nicely
C – Communicate
E- Effectively

- **SEX**

Many people use marriage as a means of satisfying their sexual desires. If your main aim of getting married is to avoid breaking God's commandment, then you are making a big mistake. You might be wondering why I'm saying so, isn't it?

Remember, marriage is not only about sex; it entails a lot more than sex, so if sex is your motive for getting married, then your marriage will just tear apart. Sex is necessary in a marriage but do not make it your main priority. So if you are thinking of marrying because of sex, think twice about that.

Sex is one of the critical parts of a healthy and happy marriage, but now due to career and daily routines, people hardly have time for it. There is usually less time for sex as relationships develop and partners take on more responsibilities. After a hard day's work, one feels too tired to touch his or her spouse. At times, one partner may want to have sex, but the other may not.

Sex is an issue many people do not give much priority to; however, it can cause serious misunderstandings in marriage. Fatigue is a common explanation offered by partners who decline their spouse's invitation for sex. Many women reject their husbands when they want sex. Remember, you're indirectly allowing your husband to have multiple partners. I'm not suggesting that you have sex even when you're tired. Some women just use that as an excuse to prevent their husbands from touching them. Women arise and take your positions so that other women do not ruin your marriage by giving your husband what you deny him.

Some men also love sex to the extent that they want to have it every day of the week. Please control your feelings for your wives need space also. Sex is important but it should not be abused, otherwise it loses its value. When your sexual feelings arouse, you can go for a walk, play with the kids, or do something energetic. You must find a way to curb your sexual desires if they are too intense and frequent. If not, it may become a habit that will be difficult to handle. If you are unable to control your sexual desires, it can affect your marriage negatively to the extent that if your wife is not available for sex, you might end up sleeping with your house help or another woman, which can end up destroying your marriage. Remember, God frowns upon adultery.

WHAT MEN OUGHT TO DO

- Take care of your wife, protect her from any external family issues, defend her when the need arises and make her happy all the time.

- Cater for your children; be responsible, giving them the needed attention, helping them to do their homework, advising and teaching them the best way in life, which is God.

- Satisfy your wife sexually, emotionally, physically, financially. Always be there for her, encouraging and motivating her when she feels down, helping her with cooking, washing and other house chores.

- Spend more time with your family than your friends. Spend quality time with your family in order for you to know the problems your family is faced with and to be able to deal with them.

- Share your goals and visions with your wife; don't hide anything from her. Let her know everything you want to achieve for she might be of help to you.

WHAT WOMEN OUGHT TO DO

Cook for your husband and children. Don't let them eat out all the time for it is not healthy. Always make sure your husband and children are fed with the right nutrients to prevent sicknesses and diseases.

Take care of the home, making sure the home is safe and presentable for your family and friends. Clean, mob, wash and tidy the home when necessary.

Satisfy your husband sexually, emotionally and physically; support him in every plan he makes, encourage him when things are tough and advise him when you need to. Don't reject him when he asks for sex; always make him satisfied in bed.

Communicate with him and the children always; this makes you able to detect when something is bothering your family. Let your family be your friend so that they can communicate with you and let you in on all that they go through.

Support your man financially when you can for it reduces his burdens and his stress level.

CHAPTER **ELEVEN**

What Ought Not To Be Done

There is rampant divorces in this age due to several reasons, some of which are gossip, refusal to perform responsibilities, ineffective communications, to mention but few. All these problems will be resolved if you follow this chapter carefully and take the decisions outlined. As married people, there is one major thing that you should not do: Do not share your private life with others. Keep your marriage life a secret from friends; it's not advisable to tell them what goes on in your home every time you meet.

- **DON'T LISTEN TO GOSSIP**

Grow up. Do not allow gossips to destroy your marriage. One will say there is an iota of truth in every gossip. That may be true; however, relying on gossip can also break the marriage. Always investigate before reacting, demand for explanation or study your spouse to know if what you've heard is indeed true or not.

Usually, when married women hear that their husbands are cheating on them, they instantly change their attitudes towards them. They become so rude and mean and even go to the extent of denying them sex, quitting house chores (especially cooking), and breaking communications. They do not even bother to confront their spouse or even study them to find out if what they have actually heard is true.

At times, you need to give your partner the benefit of the doubt. Gossip is dangerous—like a hammer, once lifted up, it can easily drive the nail into the wood and cause destruction. Gossip is also like a virus which needs anti-virus (such as trust) to purge it. Women, avoid gossip for it destroys marriages.

- **DON'T TALK WHEN ANGRY**

Anger is a normal and healthy emotion — but it's important to learn to deal with it in a positive manner. Uncontrolled anger can take a toll on both your health and your relationships. Anytime a person is angry, the person speaks words that they may later regret. Whenever you realise you are angry, try to control yourself by keeping calm and quiet until the anger subsides. Wait for your temper to cool down before you say a word.

In the heat of the moment, it's easy to say

something that you'll later regret. Always remember that words can never be taken back once they come out. When angry, take a few moments to collect your thoughts before saying anything. When your temper flares, just take a break. It's not easy to withstand someone's insults without reacting but as a Christian and a child of God, you need to have self-control.

You may want to react just to show the person that you are not a fool or that you are not easily insulted—but that won't solve the problem or make you any wiser. If you think that listening to the abusive words or being with the person who has made you angry will worsen the situation or make you react badly, take a break from the situation.

I quite remember some insulting words I used one time I got angry at my partner. It was terrible—and anytime I recall them, I feel so sad. It's not advisable to talk when angry; it worsens the situation and as such, it must be avoided. Your partner might say you're a coward or call you names but don't be offended, it's just an expression of your partner's anger. Such tormenting words can make you react—don't pay attention to such words.

I have been a victim of such circumstances that is

why I'm putting much emphasis on it so that you don't have such an experience too. I hated the word "coward" and anytime my partner offended me and I didn't react, he taunted me using that word. This made my blood boiled, causing me to use all kinds of abusive words.

Since I met Christ and gave my life to Him, I've stopped using abusive words when I'm angry. I have learnt to deal with my anger by taking a break and moving away from the situation. Let the love of Christ be seen in you, for Jesus was tempted by Satan and He could have sinned but he controlled himself. Pray for grace from above to be able to control your temper always.

DON'T SHIRK YOUR RESPONSIBILITIES

Many husbands and wives, when courting, perform all the necessary responsibilities, yet after marriage, they stop everything. People give so many reasons that I believe are not tangible. Please, don't shirk your responsibilities when you've finally gotten married.

Some husbands stop paying utility bills and providing money for the upkeep of the home with the assumption that their wives are also working so why don't they also take part in providing for the upkeep of the family. That's not the best way to go about it. You can talk to your wife and let her know if your business is slowing down and you need her help with the upkeep of the family; that's just a polite and nice way of dealing with the issue rather than avoiding your responsibilities.

Husbands sometimes deny their wives sex as well as wives denying their husbands sex in the name of work and tiredness. Well, it happens but it shouldn't be a constant excuse. On days when you're not tired, you can satisfy each other so lovingly. Do not wait for your partner to demand for sex before you do it. Study your partner to know when they're in the mood or not; this helps to spice up the marriage. Some wives wait for their husbands to demand for it before they give in— that is a very bad practice.

Some wives also use work as an excuse to stop cooking. How long are you going to eat outside the home; don't you know you're putting your health and your family at risk? Remember, catering for your husband and children is your responsibility so learn to blend the two—career and home. Do not deny your husband sex with the excuse of not being in the mood, find a nice way to present it to him, even if cuddling will satisfy him without the sex, kindly allow him.

You can also support your husband in the upkeep of the house as long as you're working; don't allow him to carry the entire financial burden. Help him to save some money by taking care of some expenses. Give out and stop being at the receiving end always. When you go shopping and you find something that you feel will look good on him, you can surprise him with that.

Most marriages break up due to such petty situations. When one becomes so selfish and stingy in the marriage, it strains the relationship. It also makes the other partner fed up and tired of doing all the work. Marriage is about giving and receiving. At times, you could also take your husband to dinner and pay for all the expenses. It makes him respect you more. If you have not tried that then start and avoid being a receiver always. You're a woman of virtue so let it show.

CONCLUSION

I still can't believe I've been able to complete this book by the power of God. It wasn't easy at all but by His grace I've made it. I always feel hurt when I see people suffering because of bad relationships they are in. Every drop of tears that comes out makes me helpless because I always want to help such people.

Through my intercessory prayers to those who are suffering because of broken-relationships and marriages, God directed me to write 'the journey to marriage' to help the young ones who are to get into relationships that would lead to marriage to take note of what really goes on in relationships and marriages.

Relationship is a period of discovering each other, building up hope, trust and it involves much work. You have to also know that true love is not only about emotions but begins with decisions-deciding that the person is worthy to have you. We don't fall in love with people per say but we fall in love with a set of qualities in a person.

Most people struggle with choosing the rightful partner so 'the journey to marriage' is written to guide people in choosing their partners. You have to know who you are before you can choose the rightful partner. Why do I say so? This is because if you know who you really are in terms of what you like, dislike, the kind of traits you want from your partner; this makes it very easy for you to choose the one you want to spend the rest of your life with easily.

It is my prayer that this book helps everyone who read it, changing their thoughts, perceptions and attitudes towards relationship and marriage. I have written this book to have impact in people's lives; amend broken relationships, help people to be on the right path to marriage, choose the right partner and finally, enjoy their relationships.

QUOTES ON RELATIONSHIP

Romance is an intimate activity for married couples, not those in relationships finding their feet to stand ~ **timewithPrissy**

True Love is not tested in a relationship but in marriage because in relationships, only good points are magnified ~ **timewithPrissy**

Love is not in words but deeds, let your deeds speak for it. Love is in deeds, not mere words ~ **timewithPrissy**

It takes only a few minutes to get married but a lifetime to build that marriage. Never rush! Take your time! ~ **timewithPrissy**

A virtuous woman is hidden in Christ. It takes a man that fears God to find and have her ~ **timewithPrissy**

Any relationship centered on God doesn't take you away from **GOD** but enhances your fellowship with HIM ~ **timewithPrissy**

You don't be in a relationship with a man because he is romantic but for the purpose he carries. Don't choose **PLEASURE** over **PURPOSE** ~ **timewithPrissy**

In fact, true love cannot be fully tested until partners are within the bounds of marriage ~ **timewithPrissy**

Who can find a virtuous woman? It takes a man that loves the Lord and walks in His ways to find her ~ **timewithPrissy**

To be decently dressed shows maturity and the rate at which you respect yourself and body ~ **timewithPrissy**

Marriage flourishes when couples work together as a team than keeping score ~ **timewithPrissy**

True love is not in the tingly feelings that shoot through you when he holds your hands or when she hugs you tight ~ **timewithPrissy**

Choose someone who sees your heart, soul, and mind, and is not afraid to point out your flaws ~ **timewithPrissy**

We live in a world where people change partners as easily as they change shoes ~ **timewithPrissy**

SEX- for pleasure and procreation in marriage but the unmarried won't leave it for the married, breeding teenage pregnancies ~ **timewithPrissy**

Motherhood is not only about giving birth, but your ability to cater for that child ~ **timewithPrissy**

Human beings have been exchanged for clothes being used, not loved! Relationship has no meaning anymore ~**timewithPrissy**

Any relationship that is not pure in the eyes of God doesn't please Him. Make your relationship pure ~ **timewithPrissy**

Adam was busy carrying out his purpose before Eve was introduced. Have you discovered your purpose gentleman? ~ **timewithPrissy**

To be a mother is a blessing but to give birth unprepared is a burden! Be ready for motherhood ~ **timewithPrissy**

After pre-marital sex, love fades, respect is lost, and time& care limits. Be wise in your relationships ~ **timewithPrissy**

A virtuous woman fears the Lord, very wise, reasonable, submissive, loyal and kind. Not every man is entitled to her ~ **timewithPrissy**

A perfect woman exist in your head, you have to cultivate her to become what you want her to be ~ **timewithPrissy**

The right relationship will lead to marriage ~ **timewithPrissy**

Men will respect you when you respect yourself as a lady. Be unique, smart, diligent and industrious. Always speak to the King in him and he will always bring out the queen in you ~ **timewithPrissy**

Any man who is disciplined in his sexual life, is responsible in every facet of his life ~ **timewithPrissy**

Men want women they can **RESPECT, ADORE** and **CHERISH** forever. How he treats you depicts how he sees you, if he disrespects you, then check how you present yourself to him. He will place value on you if only he sees you are **VALUABLE**. Carry yourselves well ladies ~ **timewithPrissy**

Real men are attracted to a woman's intelligence than her body ~ **timewithPrissy**

Friends influence your life therefore choose wisely ~ **timewithPrissy**

God designed marriage for success and only His counsel can make it successful ~ **timewithPrissy**

To understand marriage, go to God for He instituted it. Never marry without God being the head of that marriage ~ **timewithPrissy**

If a man can't be faithful to God then he can't be faithful to you ~ **timewithPrissy**

Surround yourself with good people, they make you shine ~ **timewithPrissy**

When couples highly esteem marriage, they will overcome their personal feelings and make it work ~ **timewithPrissy**

Godly marriage is a fusion, not a bond. Bonds easily split up, but to be fused in God is inseparable and unbreakable ~ **timewithPrissy**

Ignorance, immature attitudes and unnecessary arguments can destroy a relationship that will lead to marriage ~ **timewithPrissy**

Love is a minimum of emotions and a maximum of evaluating and meeting needs ~ **timewithPrissy**

Love does not hurt but expectation does ~ **timewithPrissy**

Love seeks how to make the other happy, love isn't selfish, love lives for the other ~ **timewithPrissy**

A successful marriage requires honesty, undying commitment, selfless love and **JESUS** at the center of it all ~ **timewithPrissy**

The **SECURITY** of a woman is threatened by the thoughts of another woman competing for the attention and affections of her man ~ **timewithPrissy**

A man of understanding will forever support his woman and her dreams to be fulfilled ~ **timewithPrissy**

A supportive woman helps a man to soar higher ~ **timewithPrissy**

If she can't respect you, then she's not worth having as a wife ~ **timewithPrissy**

A woman who gives you peace and a happy home is worth marrying ~ **timewithPrissy**

A reasonable lady protects your flaws but pushes you to become a better person, don't l"Each friend represents a world in us, a world possibly not born until they arrive, and it is only by this meeting that a new world is born."
–**Anais Nin**

"A loving relationship is one in which the loved one is free to be himself — to laugh with me, but never at me; to cry with me, but never because of me; to love life, to love himself, to love being

loved. Such a relationship is based upon freedom and can never grow in a jealous heart."
– Leo F. Buscaglia

"A real friend is one who walks in when the rest of the world walks out."
– Walter Winchell

"The meeting of two personalities is like the contact of two chemical substances: if there is any reaction, both are transformed."
– Carl Jung

"Whenever you're in conflict with someone, there is one factor that can make the difference between damaging your relationship and deepening it. That factor is attitude."
– William James

"When you stop expecting people to be perfect, you can like them for who they are."
– Donald Miller
"If you would be loved, love, and be loveable."
— Benjamin Franklin

"No road is long with good company."
— Turkish Proverb

"They may forget what you said, but they will never forget how you made them feel."
— Carl W. Buechner

"People are lonely because they build walls instead of bridges."
— **Joseph F. Newton Men**

"Shared joy is a double joy; shared sorrow is half a sorrow."
— **Swedish Proverb**

"You don't develop courage by being happy in your relationships everyday. You develop it by surviving difficult times and challenging adversity."
— **Epicurus**

"Constant kindness can accomplish much. As the sun makes ice melt, kindness causes misunderstanding, mistrust and hostility to evaporate."
— **Albert Schweitzer**

"For beautiful eyes, look for the good in others; for beautiful lips, speak only words of kindness; and for poise, walk with the knowledge that you are never alone."
— **Audrey Hepburn**

"You can make more friends in two months by becoming interested in other people than you can in two years by trying to get other people interested in you."
— **Dale Carnegie**

"Nobody can hurt me without my permission."
— **Mahatma Gandhi**

"As you think so shall you be! Since you cannot physically experience another person, you can only experience them in your mind. Conclusion: All of the other people in your life are simply thoughts in your mind. Not physical beings to you, but thoughts. Your relationships are all in how you think about the other people of your life. Your experience of all those people is only in your mind. Your feelings about your lovers come from your thoughts.

For example, they may in fact behave in ways that you find offensive. However, your relationship to them when they behave offensively is not determined by their behavior, it is determined only by how you choose to relate to that behavior. Their actions are theirs, you cannot own them, you cannot be them, you can only process them in your mind."
— **Wayne Dyer**

"Assumptions are the termites of relationships."
— **Henry Winkler**

"A good word is an easy obligation; but not to speak ill requires only our silence; which costs us nothing."
— **John Tillotson**

"Love is when you meet someone who tells you something new about yourself."
—**Andre Breton**

"Relationships-of all kinds-are like sand held in your hand. Held loosely, with an open hand, the sand remains where it is.

The minute you close your hand and squeeze tightly to hold on, the sand trickles through your fingers. You may hold onto some of it, but most will be spilled.

A relationship is like that. Held loosely, with respect and freedom for the other person, it is likely to remain intact. But hold too tightly, too possessively, and the relationship slips away and is lost."
— **Kaleel Jamison**

"A woman knows the face of the man she loves as a sailor knows the open sea."
— **Honore de Balzac**

"Someone to tell it to is one of the fundamental needs of human beings."
— **Miles Franklin**

"Friendship is born at that moment when one person says to another, 'What! You too? I thought I was the only one"
—**C.S. Lewis**

"The beginning of love is to let those we love be perfectly themselves, and not to twist them to fit our own image. Otherwise we love only the reflection of ourselves we find in them."
— **Thomas Merton**

"When a woman is talking to you, listen to what she says with her eyes."
— **Victor Hugo**

"Some think love can be measured by the amount of butterflies in their tummy. Others think love can be measured in bunches of flowers, or by using the words 'for ever.' But love can only truly be measured by actions. It can be a small thing, such as peeling an orange for a person you love because you know they don't like doing it."
— **Marian Keyes**

"We can improve our relationships with others by leaps and bounds if we become encouragers instead of critics."
— **Joyce Meyer**

"Love takes off masks that we fear we cannot live without and know we cannot live within."
— **James Baldwin**

"Don't smother each other. No one can grow in the shade."
— **Leo Buscaglia**

"We are afraid to care too much, for fear that the other person does not care at all."
— **Eleanor Roosevelt**

"Some of the biggest challenges in relationships come from the fact that most people enter a relationship in order to get something: they're trying to find someone who's going to make them feel good. In reality, the only way a relationship will last is if you see your relationship as a place that you go to give, and not a place that you go to take."
— **Anthony Robbins**

"The royal road to a man's heart is to talk to him about the things he treasures most."
— **Dale Carnegie**

"We often refuse to accept an idea merely because the tone of voice in which it has been expressed is unsympathetic to us."
— **Friedrich Nietzsche**

[wp_ad_camp_4]
"It is of practical value to learn to like yourself. Since you must spend so much time with yourself you might as well get some satisfaction out of the relationship."
— **Norman Vincent Peale**

"Lots of people want to ride with you in the limo, but what you want is someone who will take the bus with you when the limo breaks down."
— **Oprah Winfrey**

"What love we've given, we'll have forever. What love we fail to give, will be lost for all eternity."
— **Leo Buscaglia**

"Keep away from those who try to belittle your ambitions. Small people always do that, but the really great make you believe that you too can become great."
— **Mark Twain**

"The greatest compliment that was ever paid me was when someone asked me what I thought, and attended to my answer."
— **Henry David Thoreau**

"You can kiss your family and friends good-bye and put miles between you, but at the same time you carry them with you in your heart, your mind, your stomach, because you do not just live in a world but a world lives in you."
— **Frederick Buechner**

"Once the realization is accepted that even between the closest human beings infinite distances continue, a wonderful living side by side can grow, if they succeed in loving the distance between them which makes it possible for each to see the other whole against the sky."
— **Rainer Maria Rilke**

"The way to love anything is to realize that it may be lost."
— **Gilbert K. Chesterton**

"True friendship comes when the silence between two people is comfortable."
— **David Tyson Gentry**

"When we're incomplete, we're always searching for somebody to complete us. When, after a few years or a few months of a relationship, we find that we're still unfulfilled, we blame our partners and take up with somebody more promising. This can go on and on–series polygamy–until we admit that while a partner can add sweet dimensions to our lives, we, each of us, are responsible for our own fulfillment.

Nobody else can provide it for us, and to believe otherwise is to delude ourselves dangerously and to program for eventual failure every relationship we enter."
— **Tom Robbins**

"If men would consider not so much wherein they differ, as wherein they agree, there would be far less of uncharitableness and angry feeling in the world."
— **Joseph Addison**

"Life is partly what we make it, and partly what it is made by the friends we choose."
— **Tennessee Williams**

"Everything that irritates us about others can lead us to an understanding of ourselves."
— **Carl Jung**

"When dealing with people, remember you are not dealing with creatures of logic, but creatures of emotion."
— **Dale Carnegie**

"Three things in human life are important: the first is to be kind; the second is to be kind; and the third is to be kind."
— **Henry James**

"When you hold resentment toward another, you are bound to that person or condition by an emotional link that is stronger than steel. Forgiveness is the only way to dissolve that link and get free."
— **Catherine Ponder**

"Intimacy is the capacity to be rather weird with someone – and finding that that's ok with them."
— **Alain de Botton**

"An eye for eye only ends up making the whole world blind."
— **Mahatma Gandhi.**

"Flatter me, and I may not believe you. Criticize me, and I may not like you. Ignore me, and I may not forgive you. Encourage me, and I will not forget you. Love me and I may be forced to love you."
– **William Arthur Ward**

"What is uttered from the heart alone, will win the hearts of others to your own."
– **Johann Wolfgang von Goethe**

"Happiness is having a large, loving, caring, close-knit family in another city."
– George Burns

"What you do not want done to yourself, do not do to others."
– Confucius
"Don't walk in front of me; I may not follow. Don't walk behind me; I may not lead. Just walk beside me and be my friend."
– Albert Camus

"Having someone wonder where you are when you don't come home at night is a very old human need."
– Margaret Mead

"I like to listen. I have learned a great deal from listening carefully. Most people never listen."
– Ernest Hemingway

"Since you get more joy out of giving joy to others, you should put a good deal of thought into the happiness that you are able to give."
– Eleanor Roosevelt

"Never idealize others. They will never live up to your expectations. Don't over-analyze your relationships. Stop playing games. A growing relationship can only be nurtured by genuineness. "
– Leo F. Buscaglia

"There's one sad truth in life I've found
While journeying east and west –

The only folks we really wound
Are those we love the best.
We flatter those we scarcely know,
We please the fleeting guest,

And deal full many a thoughtless blow
To those who love us best."
– Ella Wheeler Wilcox

"A friend is someone who knows the song in your
heart and can sing it back to you when you have
forgotten the words."
– Donna Roberts

"Loving people live in a loving world. Hostile
people live in a hostile world. Same world."
—— Wayne Dyer

"It was only a sunny smile, and little it cost in the
giving, but like morning light it scattered the night
and made the day worth living."
– F. Scott Fitzgerald

"Forgiveness does not change the past, but it does
enlarge the future."
– Paul Boose

"If you live to be 100, I hope I live to be 100 minus
1 day, so I never have to live without you."
– Winnie the Pooh

"Let us be grateful to the people who make us
happy; they are the charming gardeners who make
our souls blossom."
– Marcel Proust